Baddies

DAVID STROMBERG

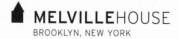

MELVILLEHOUSE
BROOKLYN, NEW YORK

Books by David Stromberg:

Saddies

Confusies

Desperaddies

Baddies

First published by Jovian Books, 2008

First Melville House printing: August 2009

Melville House Publishing
145 Plymouth Street
Brooklyn, NY 11201

www.mhpbooks.com

ISBN: 978-1-933633-76-3

Library of Congress Control Number: 2009929270

Printed in the United States of America

For their help in preparing this volume for print, the author wishes to thank: Jennifer Wang, Sabrina Bowers, Sue Griffo, Georgia Cool, Aaron Petrovich, and Margarita Shalina.

Foreword

Welcome to this collection of very very very short shorts, stories encapsulated in a sentence and a drawing. This world gets populated fast, and a lot has already happened outside the panel: manglings, bets, assumed notions about the world, ideas that have failed, ideas that have stuck, massive pain, thwarted love, genuine closeness, tar. What we see is a frozen moment in between.

Reading *Baddies* is like looking at a photography book of city characters; except it's also really not like that at all. Everything is distorted here, and from the distortions comes the realism. No one is recognizable and yet I feel an unsettling familiarity—isn't that my aunt in there? Don't I know that guy? It's a busy bus of worldly figures living on the line between abstraction and specificity, nailed down by a sentence, and their impact accumulates as you go.

Baddies is a little Thurber, a little Oulipo, some Eastern European gravitas and dread, and crates of good humor. It is a writer's-and-reader's delight, an exploration of character and change, of what's written on the face and what is not. What is fixed in us? What is fluid?

Or some better questions:

Will Minnie ever wear her petrified toes to dinner?

How is Lierre, the fox executioner, doing?

And what about the nude woman who, tilting her head, asks, "Do I seem more human to you like this?"

Does she? It could be the central question of the book.

AIMEE BENDER

PART I

PART II

PART III

PART I

The Day and Its Battle

Dima knows that he will have to
battle the orchestra again today.

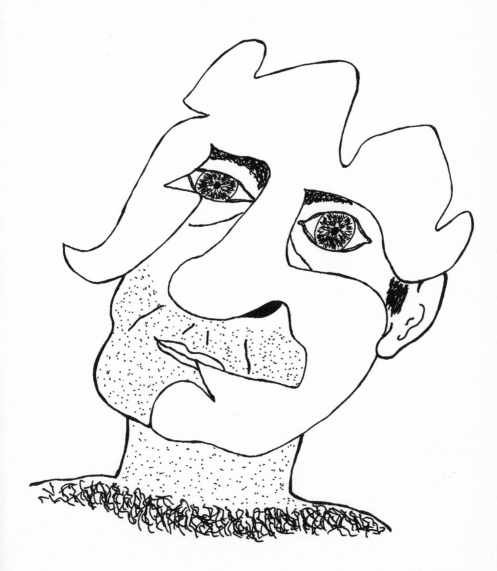

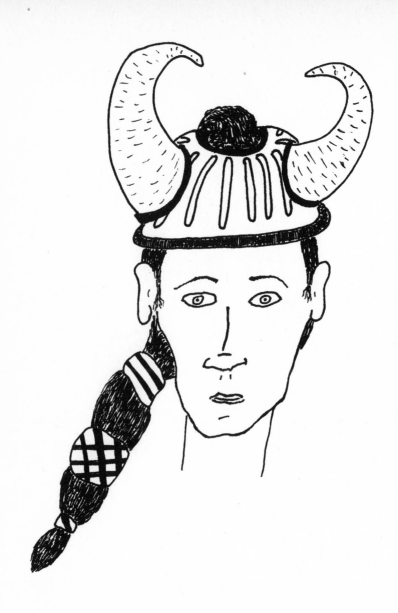

Just because Justine has pulled out
her battle armor doesn't mean she's
necessarily going back out to war.

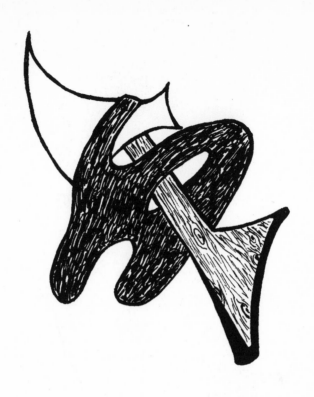

Battling ability of the highest rank didn't excuse Lufthan's inability to properly stow his chest-armor and ax.

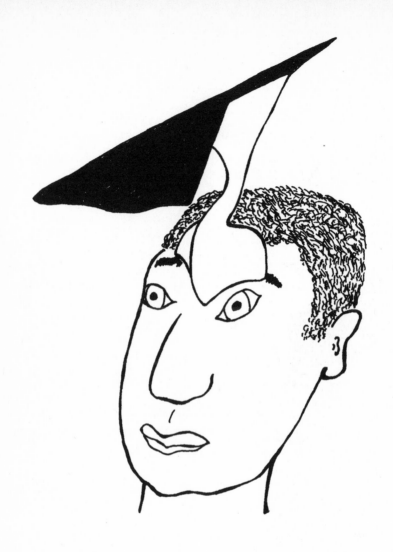

It was Lev Tochner who, donning the headdress his daughter had designed, rebelled against the Duchess's 1927 plan to expand her dog-walking territory.

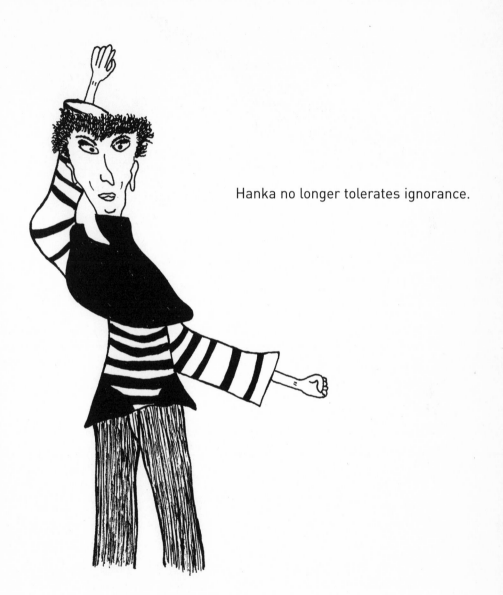

Hanka no longer tolerates ignorance.

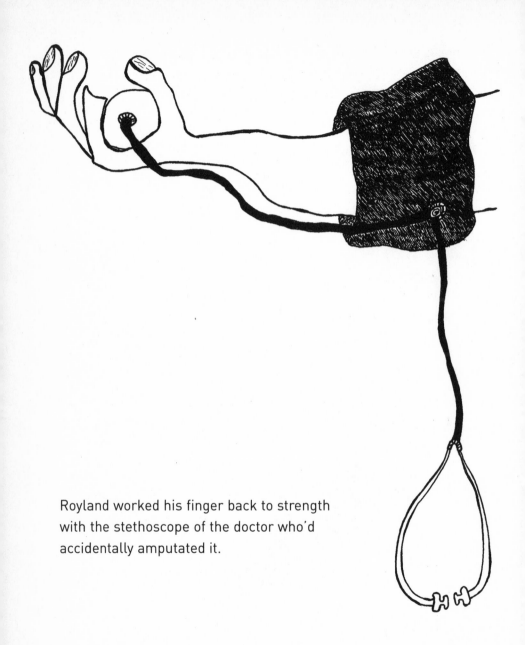

Royland worked his finger back to strength
with the stethoscope of the doctor who'd
accidentally amputated it.

Strohnschleisse's ultimate insufferability was that no matter in which direction he turned, the continent surrounding him was the same disgusting and idiotic one.

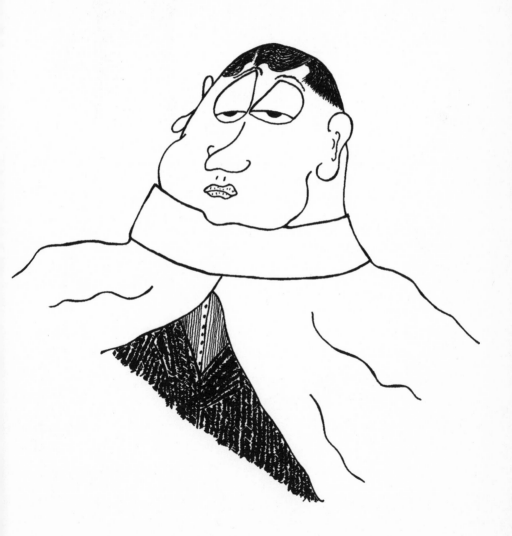

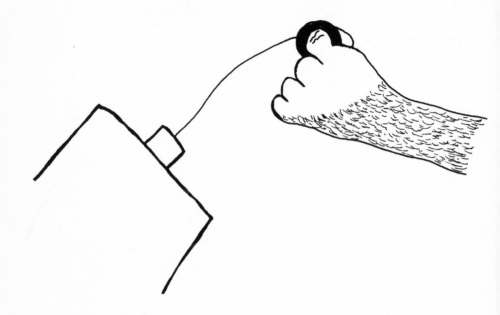

Josip *is* going to pull the tab,
which *is* going to destroy
every deli on his block.

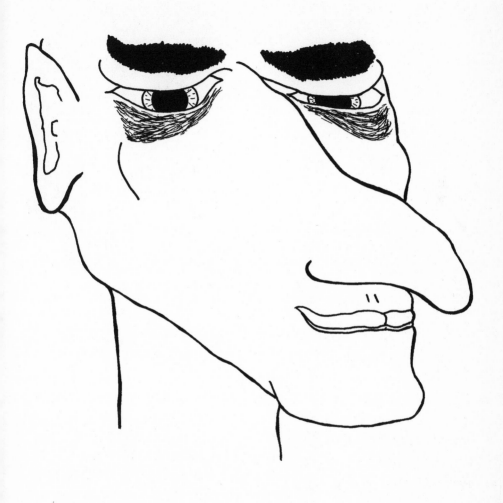

People will commemorate Haman's defeat
by eating pastries shaped like his ears.

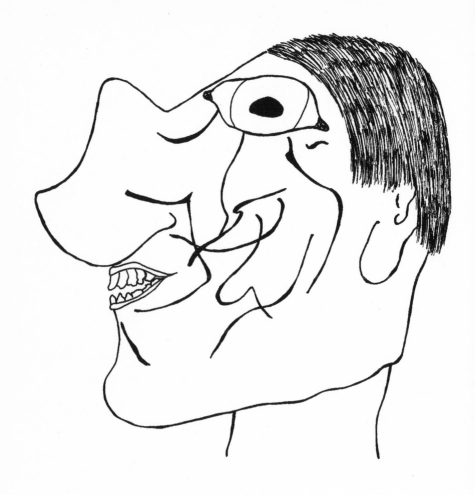

It wasn't that we found Hargon's scars hideous;
we were simply scared of a human that could
endure such mangling.

Action and Its Doubt

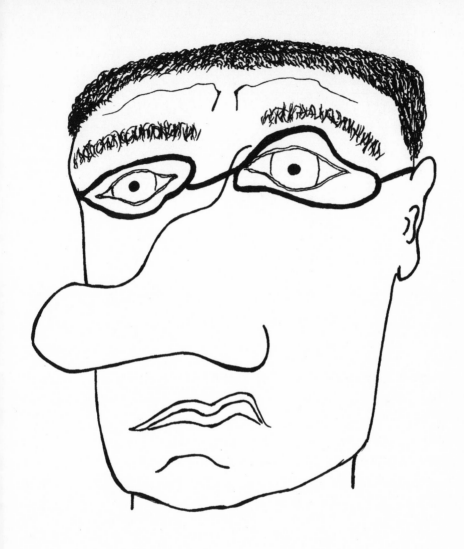

Yefim's favorite student
just asked him to teach
his most hated poem.

Celebrated for his formlessness,
Neuman sometimes felt his
enthusiasm for mathematics
exceeded his love for sculpture.

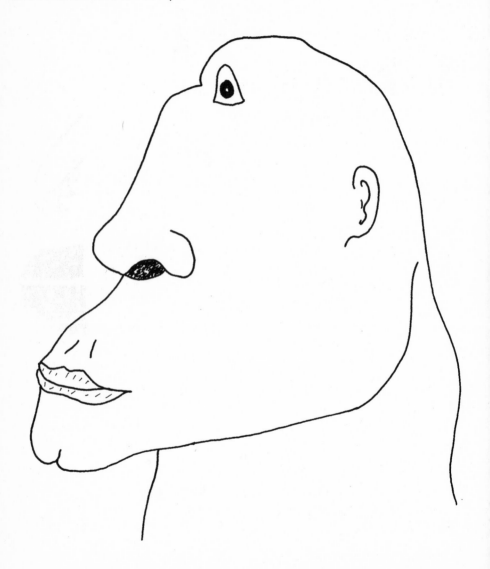

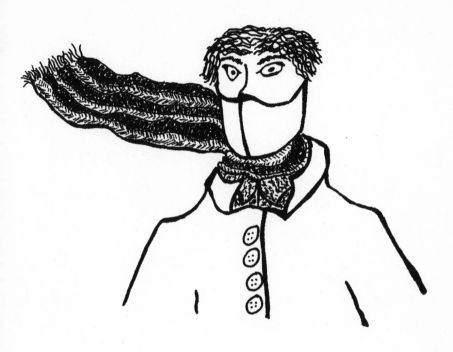

That the wind doesn't cease to blow causes
Jon to reassess his earlier convictions.

Grigor Cherny's latest composition was
anxiously improvised and performed by
the Dutch Airline Steward Quartet in the
midst of his third and final exile.

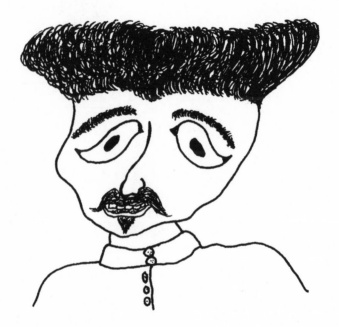

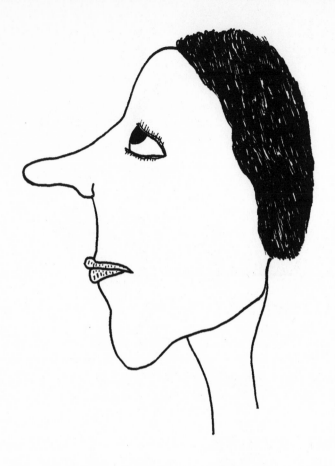

Bella refuses to concede—and until someone disproves her, her eyes will remain fixed on the ceiling.

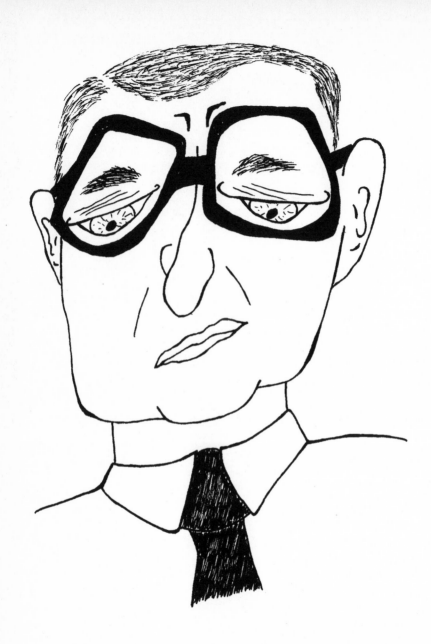

Maksim's efforts might have been
better utilized bird-watching.

Mystery and Its Carnality

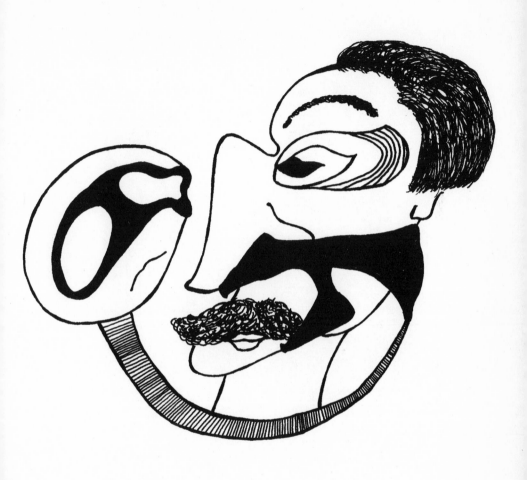

Battling the Melancholy Mustache Snatcher
was Shark-Eye's near undoing.

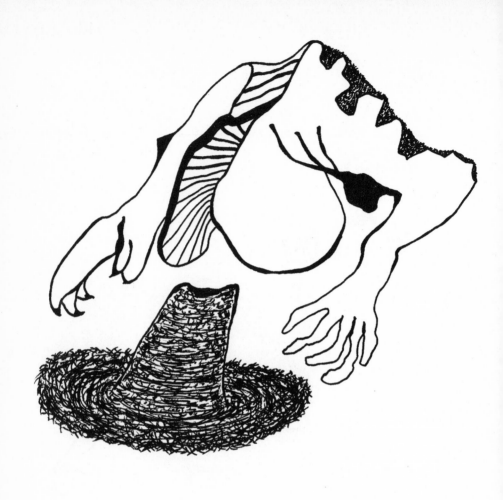

No, I can't wear that hat anymore; it's haunted
by some grave, somber moods.

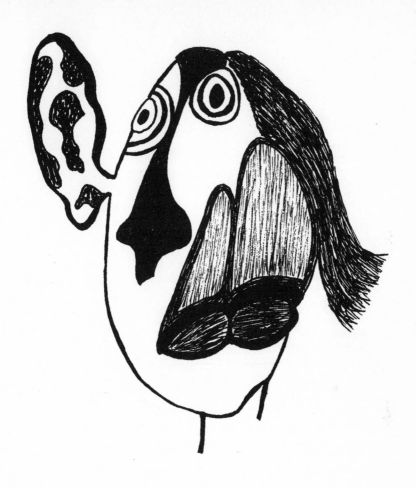

Belavia's economic model does not
resemble the general one.

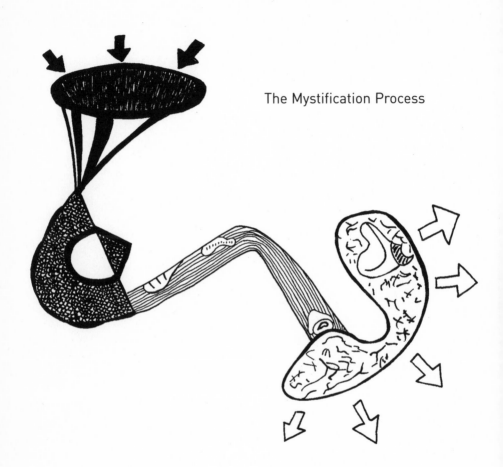

The Mystification Process

Ambition and Its End

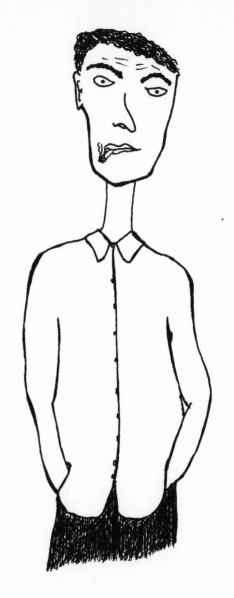

Look Vova straight in the eyes
and try to tell him he needs to
better occupy himself.

For a while, Jirka tried putting himself in
other people's shoes; when he found a
pair that fit, he ran off with them.

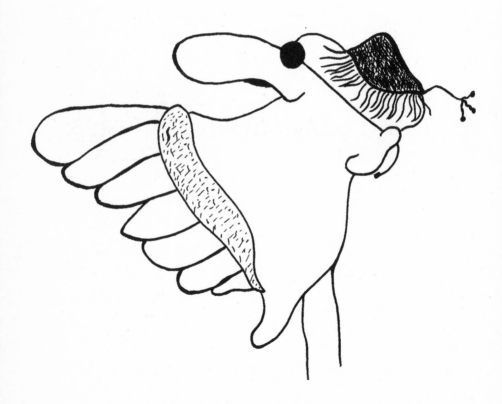

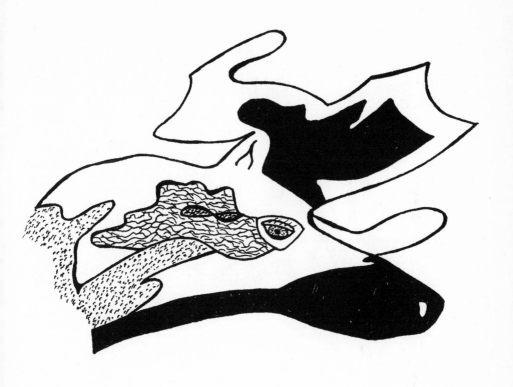

Looner yearned to physically manifest his mental landscape.

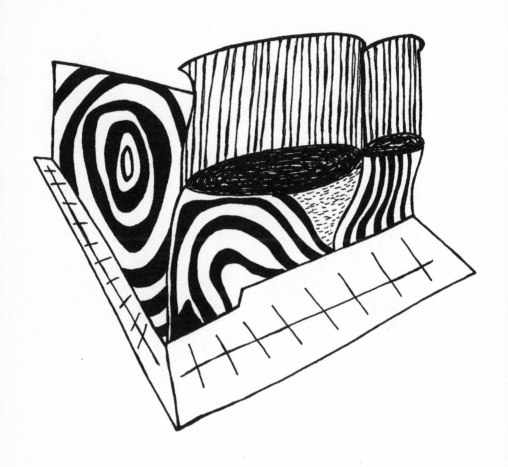

Then, as if she hadn't just spent twenty years acquiring her culinary skills, Elle quit her job and took up architecture.

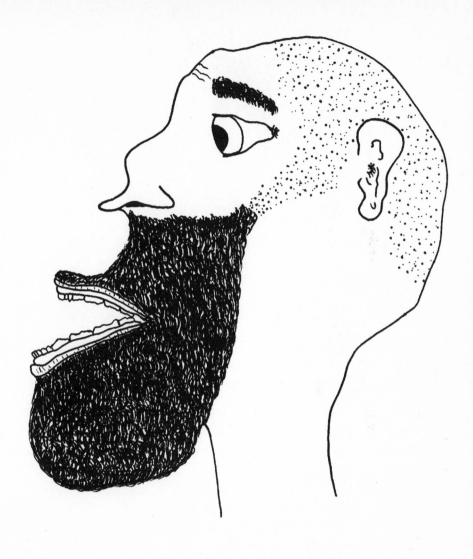

Alexei ventured to America with the sole hope that he could one day own a custom-made Persian rug.

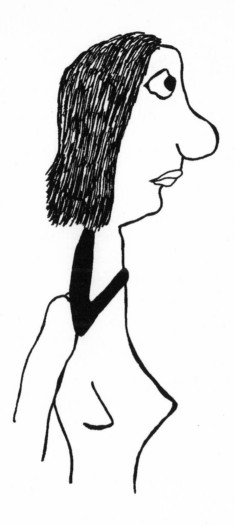

Neither of Leilani's choices is going to do her any good.

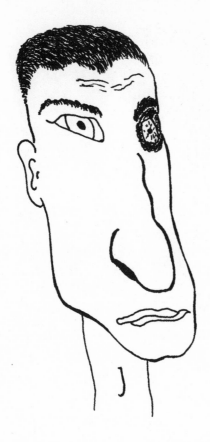

Sa'ad no longer bothers trying to restrain his natural capacity for getting into unfavorable situations.

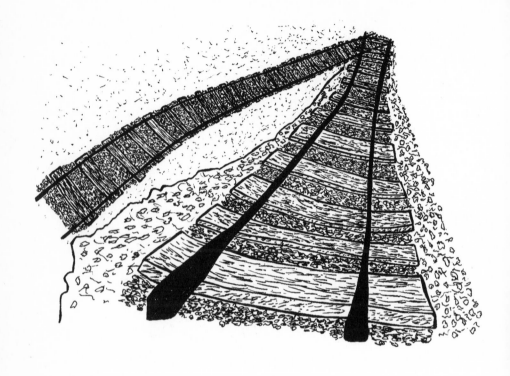

If Roman ever takes this railway again, it'll be for good.

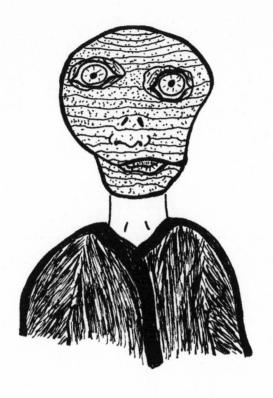

Doctor's orders: three weeks with the bandages, and then refrain from breaking beer-bottles on your head.

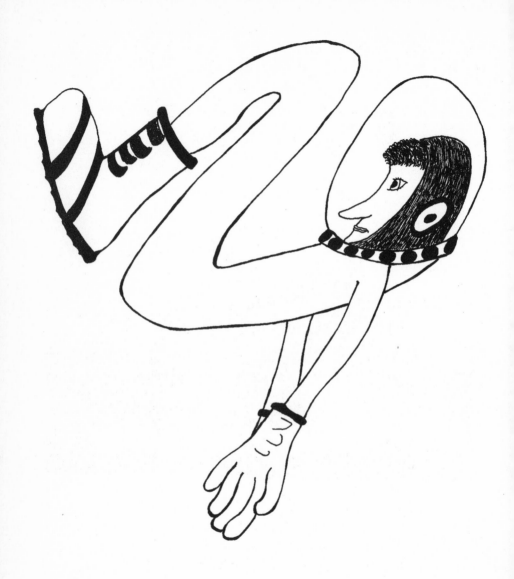

Cosmonaut Oleg Grandolovichsky has
opted not to return to the shuttle.

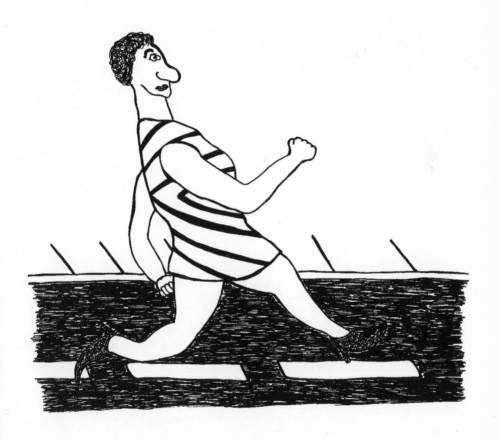

Millanne runs to work regardless of the traffic patterns.

Lottie plans to swim far beyond
the other end of the pool.

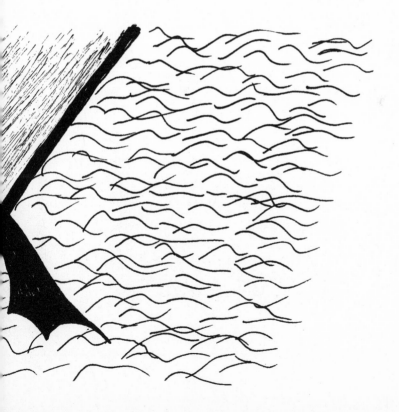

PART II

Maternal Residue

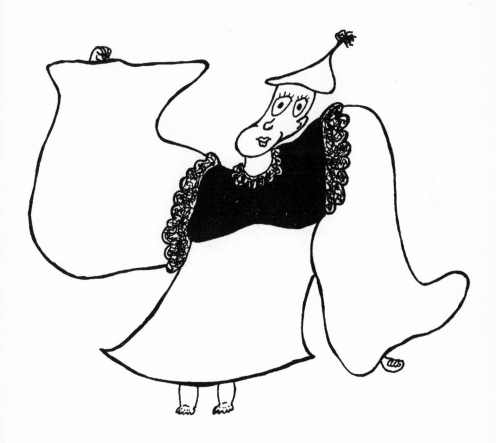

As part of the strict weight-lifting regime she started at the age of fourteen months, little Angelique shows off her muscles to Mommy every night before bed.

When Leni gave her child up for
abduction, she didn't expect he'd
be used as a pacifier.

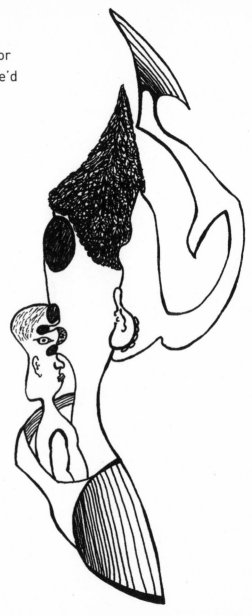

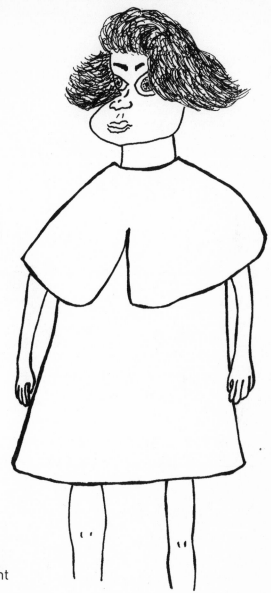

Janie's mother refuses to grant
Janie a haircut until she stops
heckling Joey Schamps.

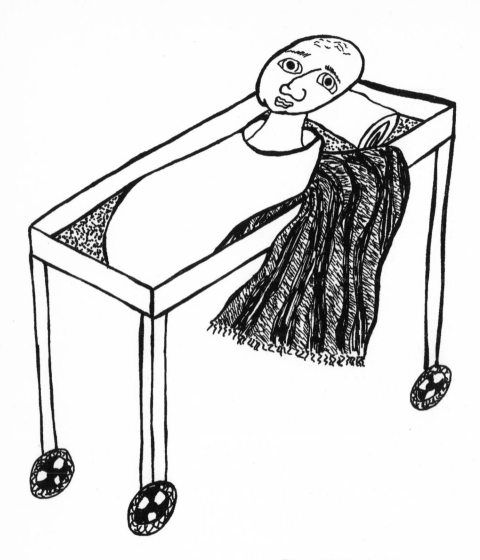

"Poor kid broke his nose
on the way out."

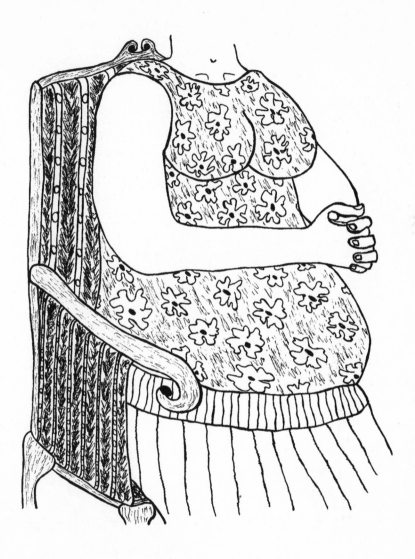

In distraught moments, Inna was a plethora of comfort.

Lina's mother was convinced that
a second-hand curtain was all the
sprucing up Lina's room needed.

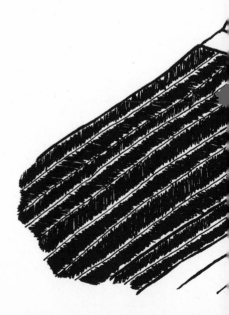

Paternal Residue

Obstructing the lower half of his perspective
with his father's bereft comb, Elogian could
comfortably ignore the ground and its
sobering materiality.

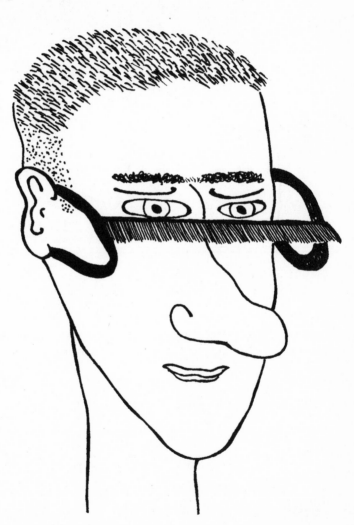

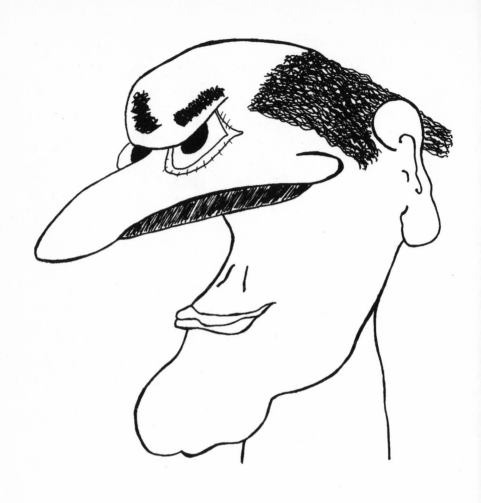

Eduardo's father's ability to handle stress
did not pass on to his children.

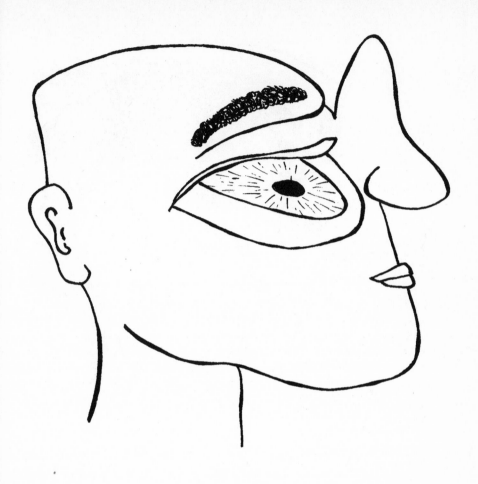

Gandilo will make an effort not to break his son's
nose as many times as his father broke his.

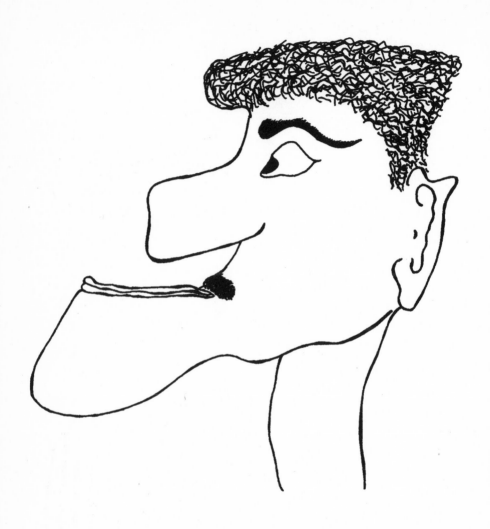

Luc-Pierre will have to be careful
not to upset himself so severely.

Today, Thom Huntson is going to inspire one or two people, and discourage several dozen others.

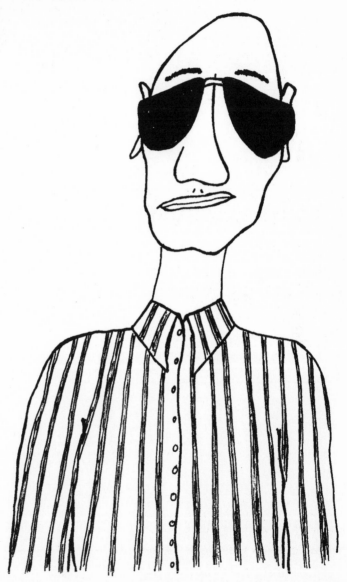

Domestic Residue

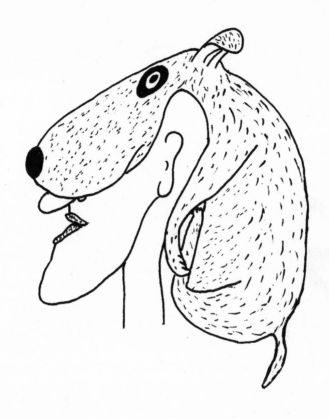

Would it be possible for me to insult
your dog without offending you?

Lauricio's butter-knife could be used only for the purpose of abstractions and abstract purposes.

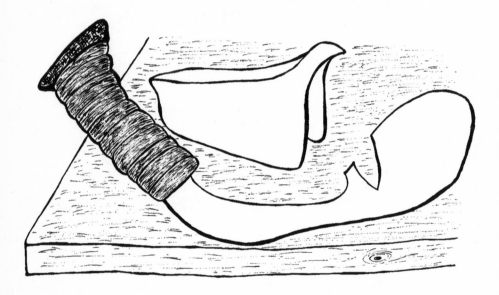

Rubinstein's glasses went missing for five hours, and somehow were returned in wearable shape.

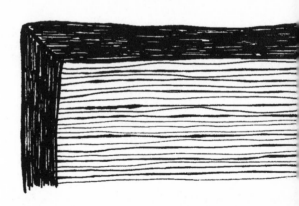

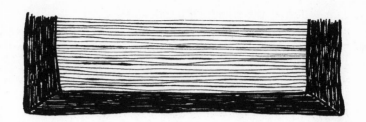

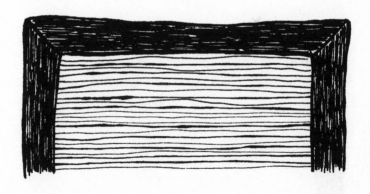

Landen will spend a few minutes hanging out
the window in preparation for a wild night.

If Madge doesn't clear the table before
the card game, the men are liable to be
thrown off track into undesired activities.

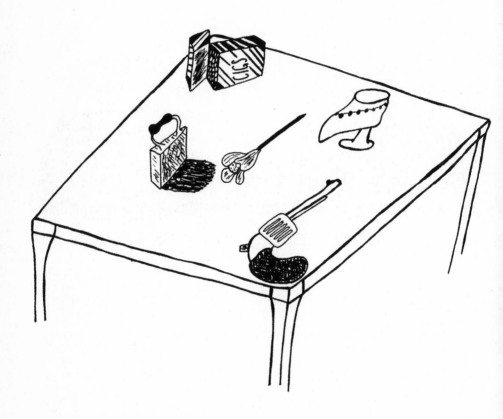

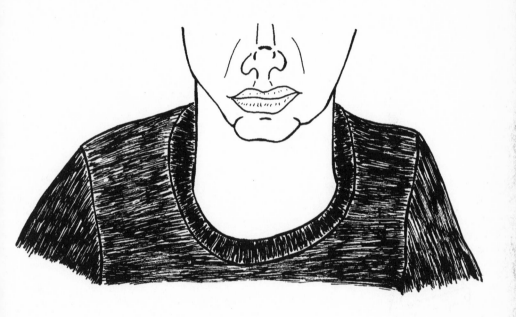

It's not likely that changing one mirror
for another will help matters.

PART III

Perversity and Its Sanctity

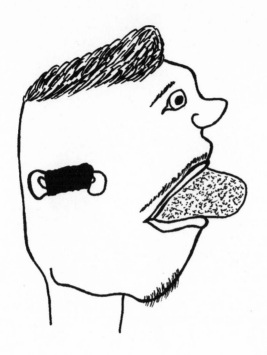

When closing off one sensual orifice
at a time no longer satisfied Martin, he
experimented with double-constriction.

Uncle Leon never divulged
how he came to possess
his single-handed-steering
mobility cart.

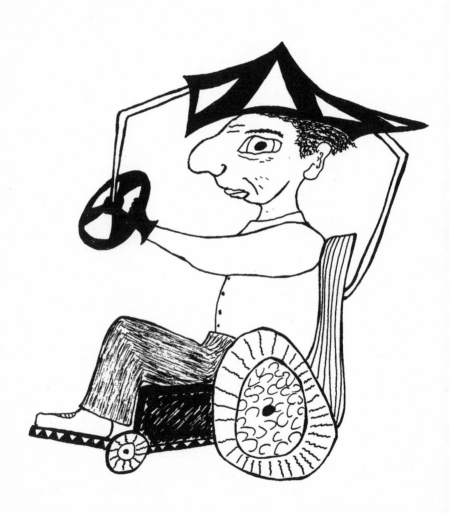

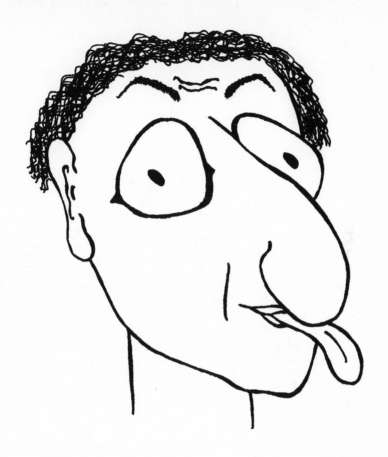

Old Neddy makes daily outings
to tease the local pigeons.

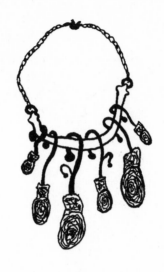

It took all the self-control Minnie had not to wear
her genuine petrified toes out to dinner.

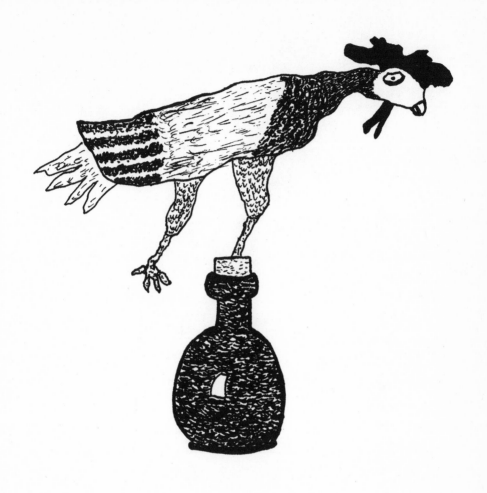

"I told you to keep him away from that stuff."

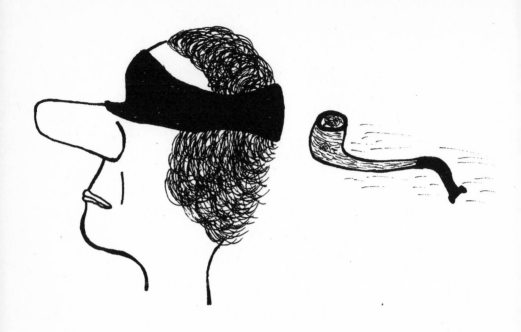

Eventually, Granny Bombo asked to be blindfolded and have smoking pipes hurled at her.

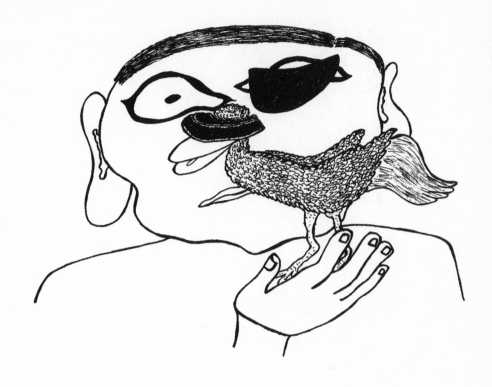

The way Lorenzo saw it, if he was going to be blind in
one eye, his pet Walbren was going to be blind in both.

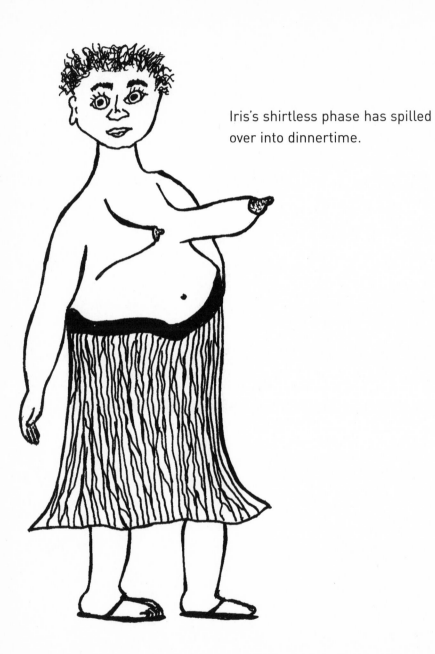

Iris's shirtless phase has spilled over into dinnertime.

Deception and Its Appearance

After a long self-imposed leave from the modeling business, Lonitta has reintroduced herself along with her *mature appeal*.

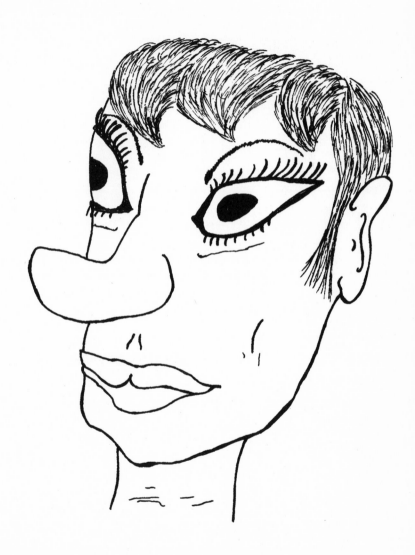

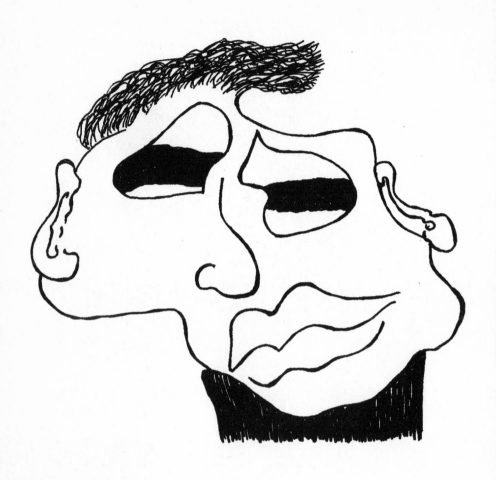

"Please tell me that isn't eye-liner
on your eyeballs."

Elan is starting to distrust his
hair-dresser's techniques.

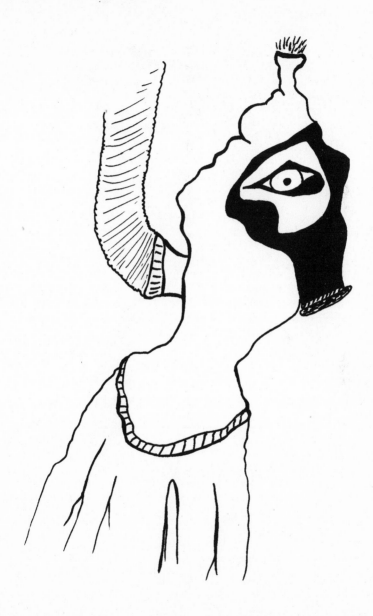

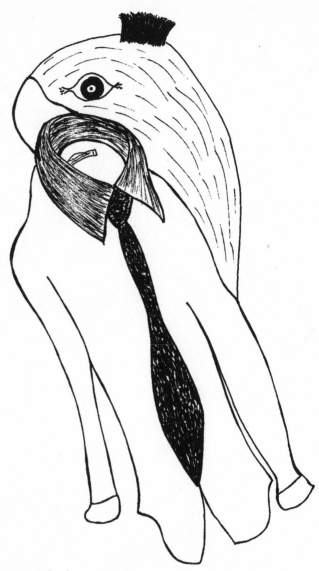

Harmon's cockatoo regularly
lunches on his office apparel.

Frankie is paying now for three straight
decades of handsomeness.

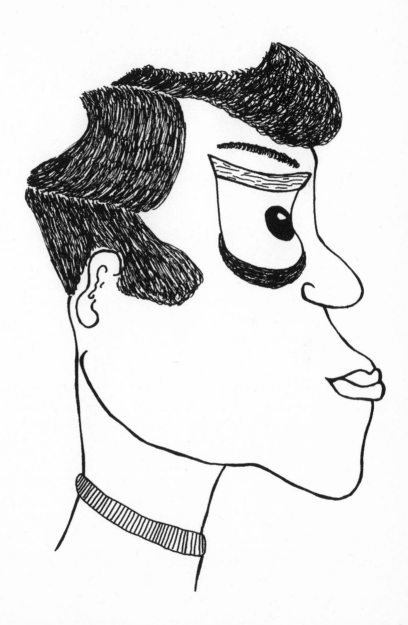

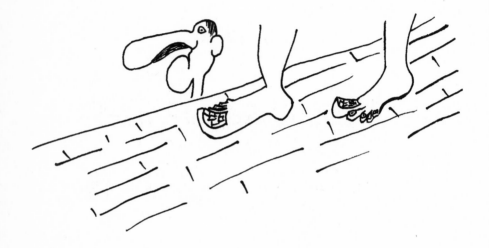

At such close proximity to the stage, Edgar
learns of the illusory nature of the theater.

And then, after he had already decided on a
hairdo, Norm found out he was not invited to
yet another ex-girlfriend's wedding.

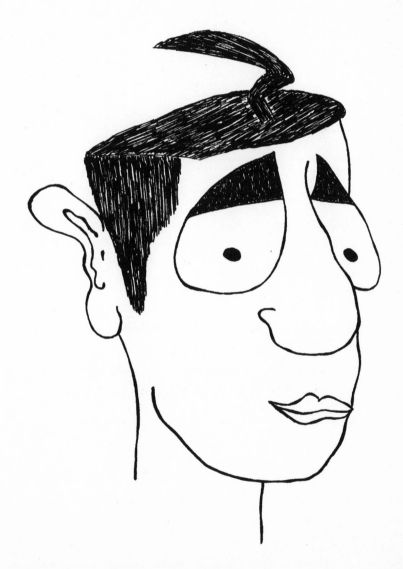

Popular neighborhood
opinion says McOro
should be barred from
wearing his signature
sweater-vest.

Sex and Its Prospect

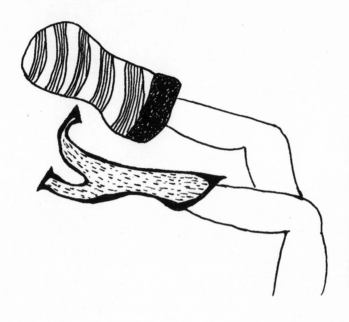

"If you want me to fuck you this way,
you have to take off at least one
style of shoe."

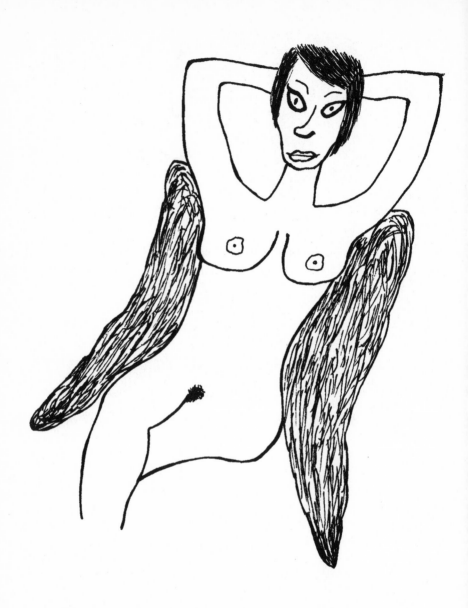

"I'm not sure I'd trust the angels in this city."

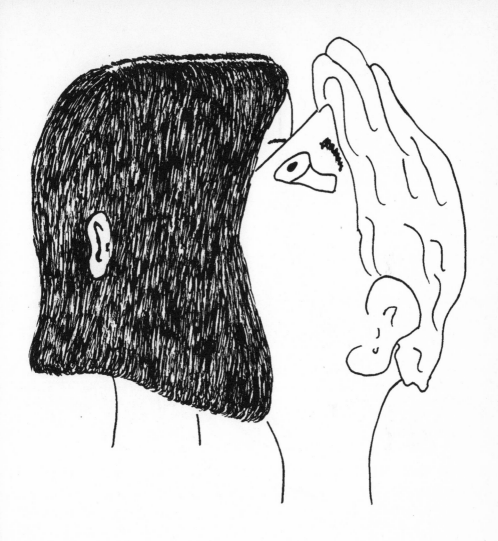

Panic strikes as Jordan tries to remember whether
he has inadvertently lied about anything.

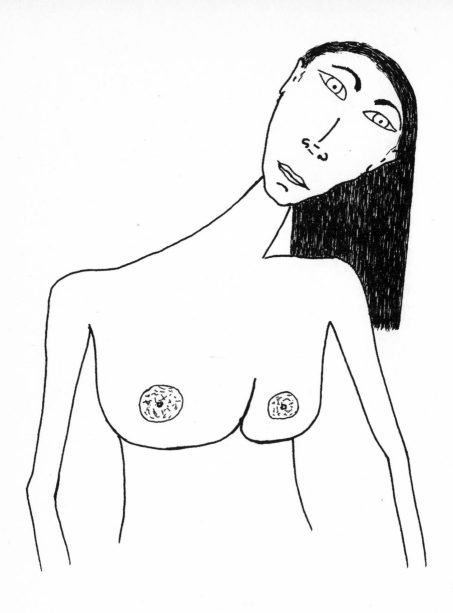

"Do I seem more human to you like this?"

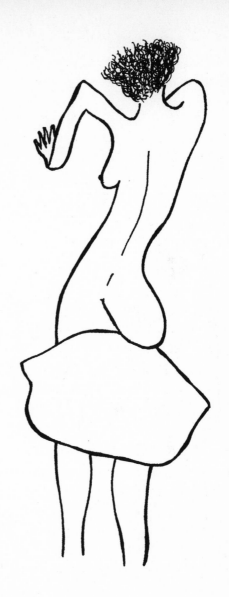

The danger of lounging around Tony's place naked is that you're liable to get just about anything stuck up your butt.

Georgette is debating whether
she wants to spend the rest of
her days as a plump woman,
or a plump man.

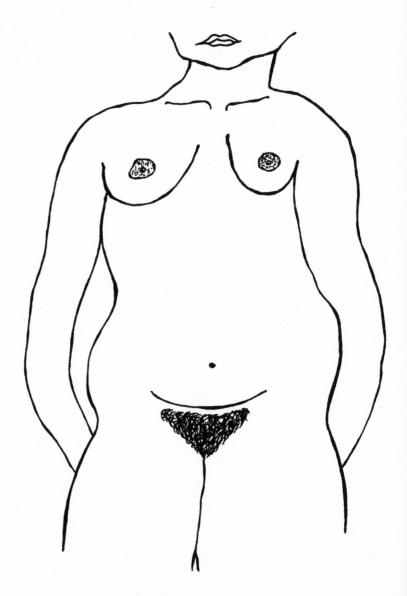

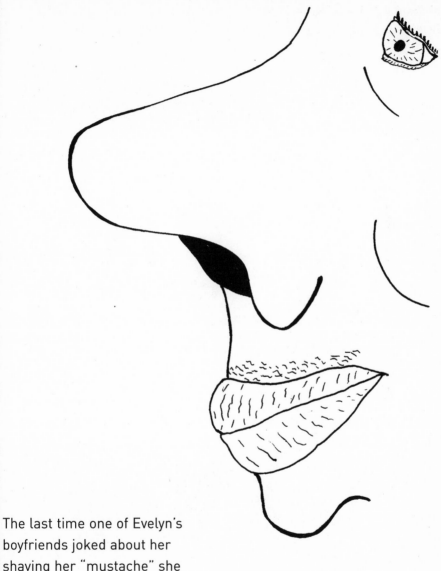

The last time one of Evelyn's
boyfriends joked about her
shaving her "mustache" she
cut him with his razor.

"If we don't turn off the lights
soon, I may remember your
infinity-eyes too well."

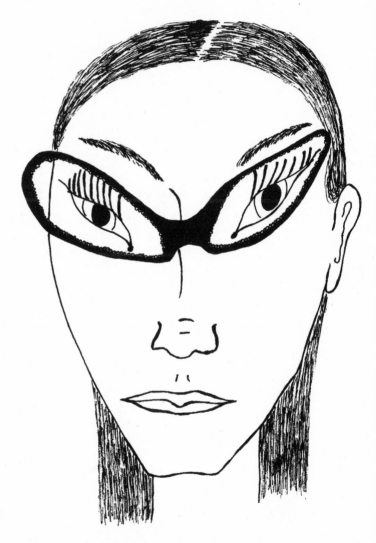

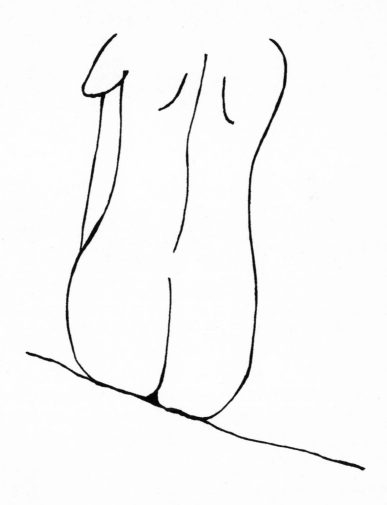

Gabriel told Yana he was willing
to sleep with her again, but that
she had changed very much.

Death and Its Inanity

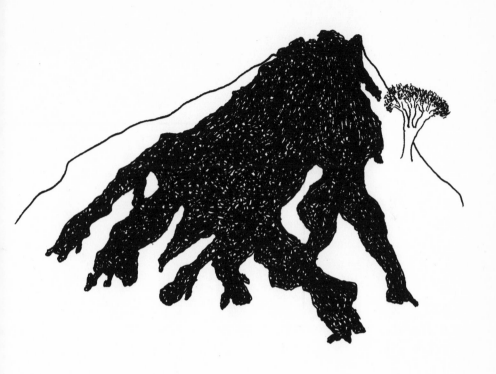

"I don't know how that tree got there, but I guess someone should've warned it about the lava."

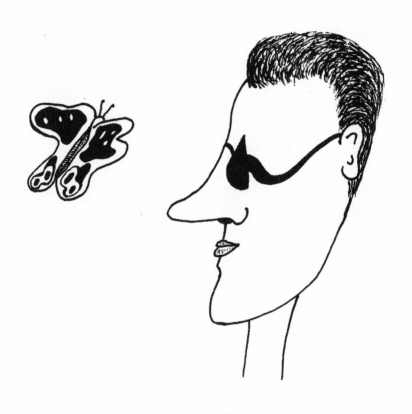

"Hermann, please ask Vlad to
shoot this thing before it tries
to land on my tongue."

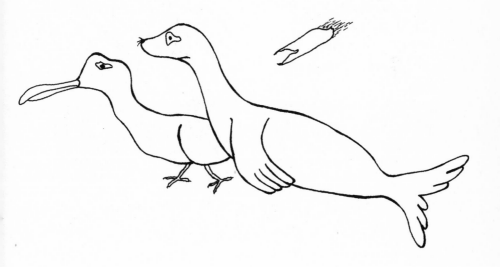

Shrapnel from the boardwalk bombing
flew to the far edges of the beach.

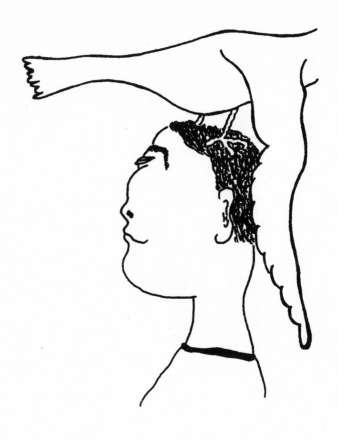

Soon after the "incident," we redirected
our efforts away from Seagull-Relief.

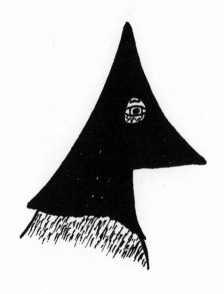

Lierre has executed several foxes he
knew to be not-so-distant relatives.

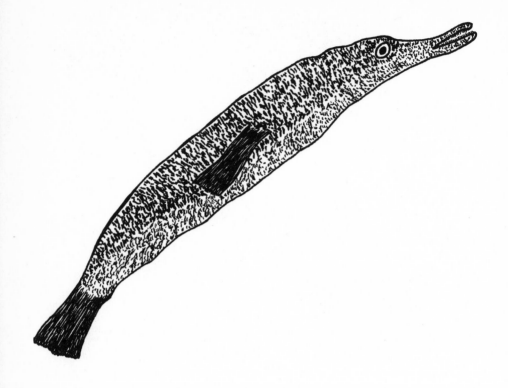

"I would've left it in the freezer if I'd known
it would thaw with such a displeasing mug."

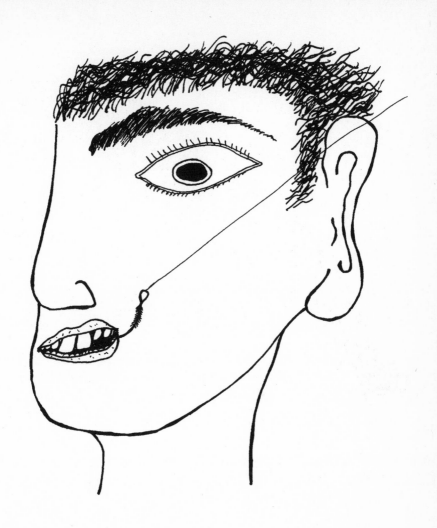

The Parkers went
fishing for pike,
but came back
with J.J. instead.

Epilogue

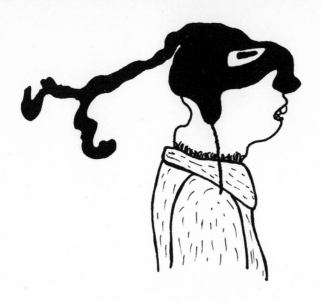

Yondele walked through the park
of his childhood, and found
it had a walkway that connected
to his first preschool.

From the grass mound he could see
the sea that stood as a consistent
promise for an end to land.

His preschool teacher, Hannah, was
on holiday, so he walked to
the old Central Bus Station and
bought a rugallach. He also found
a new candy store with the word
Šokolādes spelled out in Latvian.

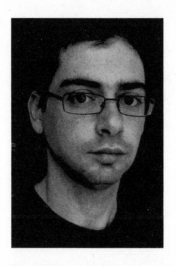

David Stromberg is a writer, artist and journal-
ist. His publications include three collections of
single-panel cartoons — *Saddies*, *Confusies*, and
Desperaddies — and he has written on art & cul-
ture for *The Believer*, *Nextbook*, *St. Petersburg
Times*, *Jerusalem Post*, and *Ha'aretz*. His fiction
has appeared in the UK's *Ambit*. Born in
Ashdod, Israel, to ex-Soviet parents, Stromberg
grew up in urban Los Angeles and currently
resides in Jerusalem.